The Fundraiser's Handbook

By

Jose-Booz PAUL and Shesly Sarepta M. PAUL
With ChatGPT

The Fundraiser's Handbook

10 Venture capital firms that invest in startups and emerging businesses.

1. Sequoia Capital - Sequoia Capital is a venture capital firm that invests in companies in the technology, healthcare, energy, and consumer sectors.
2. Accel Partners - Accel Partners is a venture capital firm that invests in early-stage startups in the technology sector.
3. Andreessen Horowitz - Andreessen Horowitz is a venture capital firm that invests in startups in the technology and healthcare sectors.
4. Kleiner Perkins - Kleiner Perkins is a venture capital firm that invests in companies in the technology, healthcare, and consumer sectors.
5. General Catalyst - General Catalyst is a venture capital firm that invests in early-stage and growth-stage startups in the technology and healthcare sectors.
6. Battery Ventures - Battery Ventures is a venture capital firm that invests in startups in the technology, consumer, and industrial sectors.
7. Greylock Partners - Greylock Partners is a venture capital firm that invests in companies in the technology and consumer sectors.
8. Index Ventures - Index Ventures is a venture capital firm that invests in startups in the technology, healthcare, and consumer sectors.

9. 500 Startups - 500 Startups is a venture capital firm that invests in early-stage startups in the technology sector.
10. Founders Fund - Founders Fund is a venture capital firm that invests in companies in the technology and healthcare sectors.

10 individuals who provide funding for startups in exchange for equity or ownership in the company:

1. Peter Thiel - Peter Thiel is a venture capitalist and co-founder of PayPal who has invested in companies such as Facebook, SpaceX, and Airbnb.
2. Reid Hoffman - Reid Hoffman is a co-founder of LinkedIn and an angel investor who has invested in startups such as Airbnb, Convoy, and Edmodo.
3. Mark Cuban - Mark Cuban is an entrepreneur, investor, and owner of the Dallas Mavericks who has invested in companies such as Cyber Dust, Jungle Disk, and Ten Thirty One Productions.
4. Ron Conway - Ron Conway is a Silicon Valley investor who has invested in companies such as Airbnb, Google, and PayPal.
5. Chris Sacca - Chris Sacca is a venture capitalist and founder of Lowercase Capital who has invested in companies such as Twitter, Uber, and Instagram.
6. Naval Ravikant - Naval Ravikant is an angel investor and co-founder of AngelList who has invested in startups such as Twitter, Uber, and Yammer.
7. Esther Dyson - Esther Dyson is an angel investor and philanthropist who has invested in companies such as Meetup, Evernote, and Yandex.

8. David S. Rose - David S. Rose is an angel investor and founder of Gust who has invested in companies such as Comixology, MakerBot, and Peloton.

9. Paul Graham - Paul Graham is an entrepreneur, author, and co-founder of Y Combinator, a startup accelerator that has invested in companies such as Dropbox, Airbnb, and Reddit.

10. Marc Andreessen - Marc Andreessen is a venture capitalist and co-founder of Andreessen Horowitz who has invested in companies such as Airbnb, Lyft, and Pinterest.

<u>*III*</u>

<u>*10 Crowdfunding platforms allow entrepreneurs to raise money from a large number of people who contribute small amounts of money.*</u>

1. Kickstarter - Kickstarter is a crowdfunding platform that allows creators to raise money for creative projects, such as films, music, and art.
2. Indiegogo - Indiegogo is a crowdfunding platform that allows entrepreneurs to raise money for creative projects, technology products, and social causes.
3. GoFundMe - GoFundMe is a crowdfunding platform that allows individuals to raise money for personal causes, such as medical expenses and educational expenses.
4. Patreon - Patreon is a crowdfunding platform that allows creators to receive ongoing support from fans in exchange for exclusive content.
5. SeedInvest - SeedInvest is a crowdfunding platform that allows investors to invest in startups in exchange for equity.
6. Fundable - Fundable is a crowdfunding platform that allows entrepreneurs to raise money for their startups in exchange for equity or rewards.
7. Crowdfunder - Crowdfunder is a crowdfunding platform that allows entrepreneurs to raise money for their startups in exchange for equity.
8. Fundrise - Fundrise is a crowdfunding platform that allows investors to invest in real estate projects.

9. CircleUp - CircleUp is a crowdfunding platform that allows investors to invest in consumer product startups.
10. Kiva - Kiva is a crowdfunding platform that allows individuals to lend money to entrepreneurs in developing countries.

<u>IV</u>

10 Private Equity firms that invest in private companies and take a stake in the ownership of the company:

1. The Blackstone Group - The Blackstone Group is a global private equity firm that invests in companies across various industries, such as energy, real estate, and technology.
2. The Carlyle Group - The Carlyle Group is a private equity firm that invests in companies in industries such as aerospace, defense, and technology.
3. KKR & Co. Inc. - KKR & Co. Inc. is a global investment firm that invests in companies in various sectors, such as healthcare, energy, and financial services.
4. Bain Capital - Bain Capital is a private equity firm that invests in companies in industries such as healthcare, consumer products, and technology.
5. TPG Capital - TPG Capital is a private equity firm that invests in companies in industries such as healthcare, financial services, and energy.
6. Warburg Pincus - Warburg Pincus is a private equity firm that invests in companies in industries such as healthcare, technology, and energy.
7. Apollo Global Management - Apollo Global Management is a private equity firm that invests in companies in industries such as real estate, financial services, and energy.

8. Advent International - Advent International is a private equity firm that invests in companies in industries such as healthcare, technology, and consumer products.
9. Silver Lake - Silver Lake is a private equity firm that invests in companies in industries such as technology, media, and healthcare.
10. CVC Capital Partners - CVC Capital Partners is a private equity firm that invests in companies in industries such as healthcare, consumer products, and financial services.

<u>V</u>

<u>10 foundations or non-profit organizations that provide funding for a variety of causes, including journalism and media:</u>

1. Ford Foundation - The Ford Foundation is a non-profit organization that provides funding for a variety of causes, including social justice, economic fairness, and sustainable development. They also fund media and journalism projects that promote social change.
2. John S. and James L. Knight Foundation - The Knight Foundation is a non-profit organization that supports journalism and media innovation. They provide funding for projects that promote access to information and engage communities in civic life.
3. MacArthur Foundation - The MacArthur Foundation is a non-profit organization that provides funding for a variety of causes, including human rights, international peace, and social justice. They also fund media and journalism projects that advance public understanding of critical issues.
4. Rockefeller Foundation - The Rockefeller Foundation is a non-profit organization that provides funding for a variety of causes, including health, economic opportunity, and urban resilience. They also fund media and journalism projects that promote social change.

5. Open Society Foundations - The Open Society Foundations is a non-profit organization that provides funding for a variety of causes, including human rights, democratic governance, and media freedom. They also fund media and journalism projects that promote transparency and accountability.

6. Pew Charitable Trusts - The Pew Charitable Trusts is a non-profit organization that provides funding for a variety of causes, including environment, health, and public safety. They also fund media and journalism projects that promote public interest reporting.

7. Bill and Melinda Gates Foundation - The Bill and Melinda Gates Foundation is a non-profit organization that provides funding for a variety of causes, including global health, education, and poverty alleviation. They also fund media and journalism projects that promote global development.

8. Media Democracy Fund - The Media Democracy Fund is a non-profit organization that supports media and journalism projects that promote social justice and civic engagement. They provide funding for projects that advance media policy and infrastructure.

9. John D. and Catherine T. MacArthur Foundation - The John D. and Catherine T. MacArthur Foundation is a non-profit organization that provides funding for a variety of causes, including justice reform, climate change, and

international peace. They also fund media and journalism projects that promote social change.

10. Omidyar Network - The Omidyar Network is a philanthropic investment firm that provides funding for a variety of causes, including economic opportunity, governance, and human rights. They also fund media and journalism projects that promote transparency and accountability.

VI

10 examples of grants or non-repayable funds that are awarded to individuals or organizations for a specific purpose:

1. National Endowment for the Arts (NEA) Grants - The NEA offers grants to support artistic projects and programs in a variety of disciplines, including music, dance, literature, and theater.

2. National Science Foundation (NSF) Grants - The NSF offers grants to support scientific research in a variety of fields, including biology, chemistry, engineering, and social sciences.

3. Small Business Innovation Research (SBIR) Grants - The SBIR program offers grants to small businesses to fund research and development of innovative technologies that have commercial potential.

4. National Institutes of Health (NIH) Grants - The NIH offers grants to support medical research and public health initiatives in a variety of areas, including cancer, mental health, and infectious diseases.

5. National Endowment for the Humanities (NEH) Grants - The NEH offers grants to support research, education, and public programming in the humanities, including history, literature, and philosophy.

6. Environmental Protection Agency (EPA) Grants - The EPA offers grants to support environmental research, education, and public health initiatives,

including air and water quality monitoring, pollution prevention, and environmental justice.

7. Department of Education Grants - The Department of Education offers grants to support education initiatives at all levels, including preschool, K-12, and higher education.

8. United States Department of Agriculture (USDA) Grants - The USDA offers grants to support agricultural research, rural development, and food and nutrition programs.

9. National Aeronautics and Space Administration (NASA) Grants - NASA offers grants to support research and development of space technology and exploration, as well as education initiatives in STEM fields.

10. The Bill & Melinda Gates Foundation Grants - The Bill & Melinda Gates Foundation offers grants to support a variety of causes, including global health, education, and poverty alleviation. They also fund research and innovation in fields such as agriculture and global development.

<u>VII</u>

<u>10 banks that provide loans and lines of credit to businesses to help them finance their operations:</u>

1. JPMorgan Chase & Co. - JPMorgan Chase & Co. is a global financial institution that offers a variety of lending products and services to businesses of all sizes, including lines of credit, term loans, and commercial real estate loans.
2. Bank of America - Bank of America is a leading financial institution that provides business loans, lines of credit, and equipment financing to help businesses grow and succeed.
3. Wells Fargo - Wells Fargo is a large commercial bank that offers a range of financing options, including lines of credit, term loans, and SBA loans, to help businesses manage their cash flow and meet their financial needs.
4. Citibank - Citibank offers a variety of lending products and services to businesses, including lines of credit, term loans, and commercial real estate loans, to help businesses finance their operations and achieve their growth objectives.
5. Capital One - Capital One is a financial services company that offers business loans and lines of credit to help businesses manage their cash flow, finance their operations, and grow their business.
6. U.S. Bank - U.S. Bank offers a range of financing options, including lines of credit, term loans, and SBA loans, to help businesses meet their

financial needs and achieve their growth objectives.

7. PNC Bank - PNC Bank is a leading commercial bank that offers a range of lending products and services to businesses, including lines of credit, term loans, and equipment financing, to help businesses grow and succeed.

8. TD Bank - TD Bank offers a variety of lending products and services to businesses, including lines of credit, term loans, and SBA loans, to help businesses manage their cash flow and achieve their growth objectives.

9. HSBC - HSBC is a global bank that offers a range of financing options, including lines of credit, term loans, and commercial real estate loans, to help businesses finance their operations and achieve their growth objectives.

10. SunTrust Bank - SunTrust Bank offers a variety of lending products and services to businesses, including lines of credit, term loans, and equipment financing, to help businesses manage their cash flow and achieve their growth objectives.

<u>*VIII*</u>

<u>*10 examples of corporate sponsors and companies that provide financial support for events, causes, or organizations:*</u>

1. Coca-Cola - Coca-Cola is a global beverage company that sponsors a wide range of events, including sports, music, and cultural festivals.
2. Microsoft - Microsoft is a technology company that provides financial support to a variety of non-profit organizations and causes, including education, healthcare, and environmental initiatives.
3. American Express - American Express is a financial services company that sponsors a variety of events and organizations, including sports teams, music festivals, and charitable causes.
4. Google - Google is a technology company that provides financial support to a variety of non-profit organizations and causes, including education, humanitarian aid, and environmental initiatives.
5. Johnson & Johnson - Johnson & Johnson is a healthcare company that provides financial support to a variety of health-related causes and organizations, including medical research, patient advocacy, and public health initiatives.
6. AT&T - AT&T is a telecommunications company that sponsors a variety of events and

organizations, including sports teams, music festivals, and charitable causes.

7. Procter & Gamble - Procter & Gamble is a consumer goods company that provides financial support to a variety of non-profit organizations and causes, including education, environmental initiatives, and disaster relief efforts.

8. Ford Motor Company - Ford is an automotive company that sponsors a variety of events and organizations, including sports teams, music festivals, and charitable causes.

9. Walmart - Walmart is a retail company that provides financial support to a variety of non-profit organizations and causes, including education, hunger relief, and disaster relief efforts.

10. Intel - Intel is a technology company that provides financial support to a variety of non-profit organizations and causes, including education, environmental initiatives, and technology research and development.

10 government grants and funds provided by governments to support research, development, and innovation in various fields, including journalism, human rights, social justice...

1. National Science Foundation - The National Science Foundation provides funding for research and development in various scientific fields, including technology, engineering, and the social sciences.
2. National Endowment for the Humanities - The National Endowment for the Humanities provides funding for research and development in the humanities, including history, literature, and philosophy.
3. National Institutes of Health - The National Institutes of Health provides funding for research and development in various medical fields, including biomedical research and public health initiatives.
4. US Department of Agriculture - The US Department of Agriculture provides funding for research and development in various agricultural fields, including food production, environmental conservation, and rural development.
5. US Department of Education - The US Department of Education provides funding for research and development in education,

including initiatives to improve student outcomes and support disadvantaged populations.

6. US Department of Energy - The US Department of Energy provides funding for research and development in various energy-related fields, including renewable energy, nuclear energy, and fossil fuel technologies.

7. USAID - USAID provides funding for international development projects, including initiatives to promote social justice, human rights, and poverty reduction.

8. National Endowment for Democracy - The National Endowment for Democracy provides funding for democratic initiatives around the world, including support for civil society organizations, media outlets, and human rights advocates.

9. United Nations Development Programme - The United Nations Development Programme provides funding for international development projects, including initiatives to promote gender equality, sustainable development, and poverty reduction.

10. European Union - The European Union provides funding for a variety of research and development initiatives across the continent, including support for journalism, human rights, social justice, and poverty reduction.

<u>25 philanthropic donors and individuals who donate money to support causes they care about, including journalism and media, human rights, democracy, justice:</u>

1. Bill and Melinda Gates - The Gates Foundation supports a variety of global initiatives, including public health, education, and poverty reduction.
2. George Soros - The Open Society Foundation supports democracy and human rights initiatives around the world.
3. Warren Buffett - The Buffett Foundation supports a variety of global initiatives, including public health, education, and poverty reduction.
4. Michael Bloomberg - The Bloomberg Philanthropies support a variety of initiatives, including public health, climate change, and education.
5. Mark Zuckerberg - The Chan Zuckerberg Initiative supports a variety of initiatives, including education, criminal justice reform, and disease prevention.
6. Jeff Bezos - The Bezos Day One Fund supports initiatives to fight homelessness and improve early childhood education.
7. Pierre Omidyar - The Omidyar Network supports initiatives in media, governance, and human rights.

8. Paul Allen - The Paul G. Allen Family Foundation supports initiatives in education, environmental conservation, and the arts.
9. Richard Branson - The Virgin Group founder supports a variety of global initiatives, including environmental conservation and humanitarian causes.
10. Oprah Winfrey - The Oprah Winfrey Foundation supports initiatives in education, health, and social justice.
11. Laurene Powell Jobs - The Emerson Collective supports initiatives in education, immigration reform, and environmental conservation.
12. Priscilla Chan - The Chan Zuckerberg Initiative supports a variety of initiatives, including education, criminal justice reform, and disease prevention.
13. Ray Dalio - The Dalio Foundation supports initiatives in education, mental health, and environmental conservation.
14. Eric Schmidt - The Schmidt Family Foundation supports initiatives in renewable energy, ocean conservation, and human rights.
15. Ted Turner - The Turner Foundation supports initiatives in environmental conservation, population control, and education.
16. Jeff Skoll - The Skoll Foundation supports initiatives in social entrepreneurship, environmental conservation, and healthcare.
17. Sheryl Sandberg - The Sheryl Sandberg and Dave Goldberg Family Foundation supports

initiatives in women's rights, education, and public health.

18. Reed Hastings - The Hastings Fund supports initiatives in education, criminal justice reform, and public health.
19. Mellody Hobson - The Ariel Community Academy supports initiatives in education, financial literacy, and social justice.
20. Elon Musk - The Musk Foundation supports initiatives in renewable energy, space exploration, and human health.
21. Hansjörg Wyss - The Wyss Foundation supports initiatives in environmental conservation, public health, and human rights.
22. Peter Thiel - The Thiel Foundation supports initiatives in education, technology, and scientific research.
23. Ann and John Doerr - The Doerr Family Foundation supports initiatives in education, global health, and environmental conservation.
24. Laurence Fink - The BlackRock Foundation supports initiatives in education, social justice, and environmental conservation.
25. Nicolas Berggruen - The Berggruen Institute supports initiatives in governance, globalization, and philosophy.

30 credit unions from around the world that offer business loans or other financial supports to entrepreneurs:

1. Navy Federal Credit Union (USA)
2. Coastal Credit Union (USA)
3. Vancity Credit Union (Canada)
4. Coast Capital Savings Credit Union (Canada)
5. Servus Credit Union (Canada)
6. Meridian Credit Union (Canada)
7. First Credit Union (New Zealand)
8. The Co-operative Bank (New Zealand)
9. Unity Bank (Australia)
10. Beyond Bank (Australia)
11. P&N Bank (Australia)
12. Credit Union Australia (Australia)
13. Teachers Mutual Bank (Australia)
14. IMB Bank (Australia)
15. People's Choice Credit Union (Australia)
16. Credit Union Atlantic (Canada)
17. Affinity Credit Union (Canada)
18. DUCA Financial Services Credit Union Ltd. (Canada)
19. Tandem Credit Union (Canada)
20. Alterna Savings (Canada)
21. CoastHills Credit Union (USA)
22. Alliant Credit Union (USA)
23. San Diego County Credit Union (USA)

24. Digital Federal Credit Union (USA)
25. First Tech Federal Credit Union (USA)
26. Patelco Credit Union (USA)
27. Security Service Federal Credit Union (USA)
28. State Employees' Credit Union (USA)
29. Workers Credit Union (USA)
30. Veridian Credit Union (USA)

30 community development financial institutions from around the world that offer loans or other financial support to entrepreneurs:

1. Accion (Global)
2. FINCA International (Global)
3. Grameen Bank (Bangladesh)
4. Kiva (Global)
5. Opportunity International (Global)
6. ShoreBank (USA)
7. Community Reinvestment Fund (USA)
8. LiftFund (USA)
9. Capital Impact Partners (USA)
10. Hope Credit Union (USA)
11. IFF (USA)
12. Coastal Enterprises, Inc. (USA)
13. Local Initiatives Support Corporation (USA)
14. National Community Investment Fund (USA)
15. New Jersey Community Capital (USA)
16. Northern Initiatives (USA)
17. The Progress Fund (USA)
18. The Reinvestment Fund (USA)
19. Rural Community Assistance Corporation (USA)
20. The Seedco Financial Opportunity Center (USA)
21. Southern Bancorp (USA)
22. Travois (USA)
23. Caisse d'économie solidaire Desjardins (Canada)
24. Réseau Accès Crédit (Canada)
25. Alternatives (Canada)

26. Vancity Community Investment Bank (Canada)
27. Co-operative Development Foundation of
    Canada (Canada)
28. Micro Enterprise Services of Oregon (USA)
29. PeopleFund (USA)
30. The Working World (USA)

<u>30 business incubators from around the world that offer financial support to entrepreneurs:</u>

1. Y Combinator (USA)
2. 500 Startups (Global)
3. Techstars (Global)
4. Plug and Play Tech Center (USA)
5. Seedcamp (Europe)
6. Station F (France)
7. Startupbootcamp (Global)
8. MassChallenge (USA)
9. HAX (Global)
10. Founder Institute (Global)
11. The Kitchen (USA)
12. Betaworks (USA)
13. Boomtown (USA)
14. The Brandery (USA)
15. TechNexus (USA)
16. Quake Capital (USA)
17. Capital Factory (USA)
18. Digital Media Hub (USA)
19. Capital Innovators (USA)
20. DreamIt Ventures (USA)
21. Healthbox (USA)
22. Nextt (Australia)
23. BlueChilli (Australia)
24. The Icehouse (New Zealand)
25. Flat6Labs (Middle East and North Africa)
26. JFDI.Asia (Singapore)

27. NXTP Labs (Latin America)
28. MEST Africa (Africa)
29. Antler (Global)
30. Accelerace (Denmark)

XIV

30 accelerator programs from around the world that offer financial support to young entrepreneurs:

1. Seedstars (Global)
2. Startup Chile (Chile)
3. Start-Up Nation Central (Israel)
4. MassChallenge (USA)
5. Techstars (Global)
6. 500 Startups (Global)
7. Y Combinator (USA)
8. Entrepreneur First (Europe, Asia-Pacific)
9. Women's Startup Lab (USA)
10. Fledge (Global)
11. Techstars Toronto Accelerator (Canada)
12. AngelPad (USA)
13. Dreamit Ventures (USA)
14. Startupbootcamp (Global)
15. GSF Accelerator (India)
16. M Accelerator (USA)
17. The Accelerator Centre (Canada)
18. Flat6Labs (Middle East and North Africa)
19. Entrepreneurs Roundtable Accelerator (USA)
20. Founder Institute (Global)
21. HAX (Global)
22. Next Canada (Canada)
23. Parallel18 (Puerto Rico)
24. Village Capital (Global)
25. Blue Startups (Hawaii)
26. Oxygen Startups (UK)
27. Seedcamp (Europe)

28. Healthbox (USA)
29. Ignite (USA)
30. Boomtown (USA)

30 economic development agencies from around the world that offer financial support to entrepreneurs:

1. Small Business Administration (USA)
2. Business Development Bank of Canada (Canada)
3. Enterprise Singapore (Singapore)
4. Innovation Norway (Norway)
5. UK Research and Innovation (UK)
6. Invest Northern Ireland (Northern Ireland)
7. Ministry of Economy, Trade, and Industry (Japan)
8. European Bank for Reconstruction and Development (Europe)
9. Department of Trade and Industry (South Africa)
10. Small Business Finance Agency (Ireland)
11. Australian Small Business Advisory Services (Australia)
12. Invest Victoria (Australia)
13. Economic Development Board (Mauritius)
14. New Zealand Trade and Enterprise (New Zealand)
15. Israel Innovation Authority (Israel)
16. Ministry of Economy (Mexico)
17. Korea Trade-Investment Promotion Agency (South Korea)
18. Department for International Trade (UK)
19. Finnish Funding Agency for Innovation (Finland)
20. Swiss Economic Development Agency (Switzerland)
21. Invest Hong Kong (Hong Kong)

22. National Research Council Canada (Canada)
23. Qatar Development Bank (Qatar)
24. Economic Development Authority (Puerto Rico)
25. Innovate UK (UK)
26. Enterprise Estonia (Estonia)
27. Ministry of Economy and Sustainable Development (Georgia)
28. Economic Development and Innovation Initiative (Jamaica)
29. Invest India (India)
30. Investment and Development Agency of Latvia (Latvia)

<u>**30 investment banks from around the world that may provide funding or other forms of support to young entrepreneurs:**</u>

1. Goldman Sachs (USA)
2. J.P. Morgan (USA)
3. Morgan Stanley (USA)
4. Credit Suisse (Switzerland)
5. Deutsche Bank (Germany)
6. Barclays (UK)
7. Citigroup (USA)
8. UBS (Switzerland)
9. HSBC (UK)
10. Nomura (Japan)
11. BNP Paribas (France)
12. Societe Generale (France)
13. Bank of America Merrill Lynch (USA)
14. Jefferies (USA)
15. Lazard (USA)
16. Rothschild & Co (Global)
17. Evercore (USA)
18. Moelis & Company (USA)
19. Piper Sandler (USA)
20. RBC Capital Markets (Canada)
21. Macquarie Group (Australia)
22. Itau BBA (Brazil)
23. China International Capital Corporation (China)
24. Standard Chartered (UK)
25. Daiwa Securities (Japan)
26. Mizuho Financial Group (Japan)
27. Nomura Holdings (Japan)

28. Banco Santander (Spain)
29. Sumitomo Mitsui Financial Group (Japan)
30. Mitsubishi UFJ Financial Group (Japan)

<u>*30 media companies funds from around the world that may provide financial support to entrepreneurs:*</u>

1. Comcast Ventures (USA)
2. Hearst Ventures (USA)
3. Bertelsmann Digital Media Investments (Germany)
4. Advance (USA)
5. Time Warner Investments (USA)
6. News Corp. (USA)
7. Verizon Ventures (USA)
8. Viacom Ventures (USA)
9. Bertelsmann Investments (Germany)
10. Gannett Ventures (USA)
11. Condé Nast (USA)
12. Axel Springer Digital Ventures (Germany)
13. Discovery Communications (USA)
14. ProSiebenSat.1 (Germany)
15. New York Times Company (USA)
16. Tribune Media Ventures (USA)
17. Mediaset (Italy)
18. Naspers Ventures (South Africa)
19. ITV Ventures (UK)
20. TF1 Group (France)
21. HearstLab (USA)
22. Disney Accelerator (USA)
23. Bertelsmann Content Investments (Germany)
24. CBS Ventures (USA)
25. Roularta Media Group (Belgium)
26. Bloomberg Beta (USA)
27. Sinclair Broadcast Group (USA)

28. Future plc (UK)
29. Bonnier Ventures (Sweden)
30. NHST Media Group (Norway)